ASUNCION

BY JESSE EISENBERG

★

★

DRAMATISTS
PLAY SERVICE
INC.

ASUNCION received its Off-Broadway premiere at the Cherry Lane Theater on October 27, 2011. It was presented by Rattlestick Playwrights Theater (David van Asselt, Artistic Director; Brian Long, Managing Director). It was directed by Kip Fagan; the set design was by John McDermott; the costume design was by Jessica Pabst; the lighting design was by Ben Stanton; the sound design was by Bart Fasbender; the production stage manager was Melissa Mae Gregus; the production manager was Eugenia Furneaux; the fight director was Thomas Schall; and the technical director was Katie Takacs. The cast was as follows:

STUART . . . . Remy Auberjonois
VINNY . . . . Justin Bartha
EDGAR . . . . Jesse Eisenberg
ASUNCION . . . . Camille Mana

CHARACTERS

STUART

VINNY

EDGAR

ASUNCION

ASUNCION

ACT ONE

Scene 1

A claustrophobic attic apartment, off-campus in Binghamton, New York. The ceiling sinks inward. In the main room, a Pan-African flag covers a ratty couch. A small kitchen is off to the left, the sink full.

A large window is upstage center but is covered by a map of the world with the colorful heading, "Where Are We?"

Off stage left is a bedroom, off stage right, a bathroom and upstage, the entrance to the house.

Vinny plays the blues on a Casio keyboard. A small, lit joint sits on the keyboard. Vinny takes a hit and continues playing.

Edgar enters, shouldering a bicycle. His face is dripping with blood. Vinny does not look up, still playing the blues.

VINNY. You got some African shit right here. Some African shit right here. You got Africa, a bit of Bamako and the Niger Delta, then straight around the horn and up the crack of the Mississippi Delta. You got ragtime, call and response, Memphis, St. Louis, and then up the crack of the queen, Bessie Smith. That's what the fucking blues is. *(Sings with the music.)* "Let it be known … Let it be told … " You got some African shit, right here.
EDGAR. Yeah? I didn't know that. I didn't know that about the blues.

VINNY. "Sure as fire … "

EDGAR. I thought it was more of a domestic — a domestic tradition.

VINNY. Fuck, man. The blues originated in West Africa.

EDGAR. Huh. I didn't realize. You have, like, such specific knowledge, which is so great.

VINNY. "Quick as the sun … "

EDGAR. Do you teach the blues in your class? To your other students?

VINNY. I teach it in *life,* man.

EDGAR. Oh. Okay.

VINNY. The blues are a feeling. The actual music is just paper. "Tellin' the doctor not to visit … "

EDGAR. Right, that's a good point. Do you know where in West Africa?

VINNY. "Pleasin' to the eye … "

EDGAR. 'Cause I was thinking of traveling to The Gambia, which is actually a tiny country completely tucked inside Senegal.

VINNY. They're just holding hands, man.

EDGAR. And there's a food shortage there. So I thought I could be of use.

VINNY. *(Playing.)* They got everything they need right here.

EDGAR. Did you want some more water? I sometimes feel thirsty even when I'm totally hydrated. They say if you feel thirsty, you're already dehydrated. I'm gonna get a glass. Do you want one?

VINNY. "And equal to the ladies … "

EDGAR. I'll refill yours.

VINNY. Thanks, man.

EDGAR. Of course. Keep playing. It's good. I'm entertained. *(Edgar enters the kitchen and turns on the faucet.)* I'm letting it run so it's cold. I know you like it cold. *(Brings water to Vinny.)* Your water, *monsieur.*

VINNY. All right, settle down. *(Vinny notices Edgar's bloody face.)* Edgar.

EDGAR. Yes?

VINNY. You're bleeding.

EDGAR. Am I?

VINNY. Your whole face, your whole face is bleeding completely.

EDGAR. Yeah? Am I, is it still bleeding? *(Touching his face.)* Huh. I wasn't sure.

6

VINNY. What the hell happened to you?

EDGAR. It was strange, actually. I had a strange night.

VINNY. Jesus Christ, Edgar!

EDGAR. I'm sorry — I should've cleaned it.

VINNY. How are you gonna clean it? I'll clean it. Shit, sit down. *(Edgar sits, Vinny fetches a towel.)* Jesus, what am I gonna do with you?

EDGAR. I don't know.

VINNY. Can you tell me what happened?

EDGAR. Yeah, it's really nothing. I got attacked a little bit. Can you say it again?

VINNY. What?

EDGAR. You know — "What am I gonna…?"

VINNY. What am I gonna do with you?

EDGAR. *(Delighted.)* I don't know, I don't know!

VINNY. Okay, put your head back.

EDGAR. Sure, thanks. You don't have to do this, I could clean it. I could do it myself later.

VINNY. Put your head back. *(Cleans the wound.)* Does it hurt?

EDGAR. No, you have a gentle touch.

VINNY. So what happened?

EDGAR. I was biking down by Frank's to get your sandwich and some kids — they were just playing around really, it wasn't malicious — but they kind of pushed me off the bike and slammed me into a concrete pillar. And my face slammed into the wall and I think I passed out or something. I don't remember.

VINNY. Did you see who they were?

EDGAR. No, they struck me right in my eyes. But they seemed harmless. I'm really fine. And — the good news. *(Pulls out his wallet.)* Still got my wallet!

VINNY. *(Sarcastic.)* That is good news!

EDGAR. The money is missing, but I still have my license, my Social Security card — that stuff is a pain to get back, if you lose it.

VINNY. So it's a win-win, really.

EDGAR. But I seem to have lost my cell phone.

VINNY. You lost it?

EDGAR. Yeah, I can't seem to find it — you didn't see it anywhere around here, did you?

VINNY. *(Like he's an idiot.)* Edgar, maybe while you were unconscious, after you were attacked and while your money was being

7

stolen from you, the kids took your cell phone. Maybe you didn't just leave it home.

EDGAR. I don't want to jump to conclusions.

VINNY. You were attacked, Edgar, and robbed. I think it's okay to assume they took your phone.

EDGAR. That's ... Vinny, that's a little racist.

VINNY. How is it racist?

EDGAR. To assume that they just took the phone because they're black.

VINNY. You never told me that they were black.

EDGAR. *(Beat.)* Even so.

VINNY. I have a fucking masters in Black Studies!

EDGAR. So that absolves you of being racist?

VINNY. Fuck you.

EDGAR. Sorry.

VINNY. Fuck you, Edgar!

EDGAR. Okay. I'm sorry, I'm a little shaken up, understandably. I'm a little anxious, Vinny. Understandably. I'm just — I feel like an idiot.

VINNY. *(Gently touching Edgar's wound.)* It'll be character-building.

EDGAR. You've been up to the First Ward, you see how they live. They're oppressed by everything. Every food stamp banner and pothole and broken window, you know? Every missing tooth and every amputee and the pregnant teenage girls still wearing the short skirts trying to be sexy seven months in, like, as soon as this one comes out, I'm ready for another. And ... it's embarrassing and ... and I would punch me too! I would punch me, Vinny. I would do something to me, I would.

VINNY. No, you wouldn't.

EDGAR. I would — I feel like an idiot. I'm like a walking white idiot or something.

VINNY. You're just young.

EDGAR. I know.

VINNY. And naive.

EDGAR. I know.

VINNY. And also ignorant. *(Vinny pushes Edgar's head, slamming it forward.)*

EDGAR. Jesus, Vinny!

VINNY. You're naïve, Edgar. And it's offensive.

EDGAR. I know. I know I am.

VINNY. You gotta learn to fight back a little bit.

EDGAR. You think so?

VINNY. "Nonviolence is fine as long as it works."

EDGAR. Muhammad Ali?

VINNY. *(Shakes his head.)* Malcolm X. Intended sarcastically.

EDGAR. I think you're a genius. *(Vinny stands abruptly.)*

VINNY. I gotta grade papers.

EDGAR. I can grade them for you.

VINNY. I don't need you to grade them —

EDGAR. But you love my comments and I still have the red pen!

VINNY. You should do something of your own.

EDGAR. Okay.

VINNY. I'm becoming impatient. Just do something normal. Turn the radio on for a minute. Jerk off into a sock or something.

EDGAR. *(Blushing.)* Come on, don't say that. It's inappropriate. You're my teacher.

VINNY. I was your T.A., one semester, three years ago; we move on. Why don't you work on something?

EDGAR. I can't … I'm bored … please, I know.

VINNY. You know? Okay. 'Cause I would like some rent eventually.

EDGAR. Is it the first of the month already?

VINNY. It's May 17th.

EDGAR. Oh. Well, I would like to pay it, believe you me. I'll get back on it, I promise. I'm looking for a story. I'm on the prowl!

VINNY. Why don't you write about the kids that hurt you? It's a good story. All the economic disparity bullshit. I'll submit it to the school paper if you want.

EDGAR. Yeah, maybe. Maybe, I don't know. I'm too close to it, I think. I'm too close to it.

VINNY. Right.

EDGAR. And the pay is shit.

VINNY. Right.

EDGAR. But it's a good suggestion. I appreciate it.

VINNY. *(Didactic.)* Don't be glib, Edgar. Good night. *(Vinny begins to exit as a cell phone rings, playing "Für Elise.")*

EDGAR. Vinny. Do you hear that?

VINNY. Yes, it's Beethoven's "Für Elise."

EDGAR. No, I mean my phone — *(Edgar reaches under the couch and pulls out his cell phone.)* You see? I left it home.

VINNY. Huh.

EDGAR. So they only took my money.

VINNY. I was too harsh on them, then. Who's calling you?

EDGAR. It's Sherry again.

VINNY. You gonna answer it?

EDGAR. Should I?

VINNY. It's a free country.

EDGAR. I'm not going to.

VINNY. Why? Because she's fat?

EDGAR. No.

VINNY. But she is fat, Edgar. Don't be a liar. *(Vinny grabs his joint and crosses offstage into his bedroom. Edgar stares at his phone as the Beethoven ring continues to play. Blackout.)*

Scene 2

The next morning.

Edgar lies on a beanbag chair on the floor, reading. The apartment buzzer rings. Edgar ignores it. It rings again. And again. Edgar ignores it. One final sustained buzz and Edgar moves to the intercom, presses it.

EDGAR. Yeah?

STUART. *(Offstage.)* Edgar!

EDGAR. Hello?

STUART. *(Offstage.)* It's me.

EDGAR. Who's "me," please?

STUART. *(Offstage.)* Just buzz me up, douchebag.

EDGAR. Stuart?

STUART. *(Offstage.)* Buzz me up. *(Edgar hits the buzzer and goes back to the beanbag. Stuart enters, in a suit.)* There's a homeless guy sitting outside your building.

EDGAR. Yeah, Terry.

STUART. You know his name?

EDGAR. Yes, it's Terry. I hope you gave him money, he's frequently hungry.

STUART. I was polite, don't worry.

EDGAR. It's good to see you haven't changed, Stuart.

STUART. *(Looking around the room.)* You too.

EDGAR. I take that as a compliment.

STUART. You shouldn't. Can I sit down?

EDGAR. What are you doing here?

STUART. I need a reason to visit you? Is Vinny here?

EDGAR. He's teaching a class. He'll be home in twenty minutes, if he doesn't get his sandwich.

STUART. Fine, that'll be fine. What the hell is this? *(Stuart has sat on Edgar's cell phone.)*

EDGAR. My cell. I charge it while Vinny's at class.

STUART. This place is even worse than I remember.

EDGAR. We've made some changes, mainly for a different feng shui. And I retiled the kitchen last winter.

STUART. You shouldn't live like this, you're smart, you could have a good life. I could loan you money, Mom could loan you money.

EDGAR. Mom's a vegetable and I don't need your blood money, thank you very much. Anyway, we define "good" differently, Stuart. I'm on a path, it's important for me to be here right now.

STUART. You're sleeping on a beanbag, dude, and trust me, I like Vinny, I really do, but he's your teacher —

EDGAR. Don't be ridiculous; he was my T.A. for one semester like a bazillion years ago; we've both moved on. It's totally a peer relationship now. Can I get you some water, Stuart?

STUART. It's a little gay, though, don't you think?

EDGAR. Okay, thank you for not being sexual, Stuart! I'd like to get you some water —

STUART. It's not healthy, Edgar. Vinny is an adult and you're —

EDGAR. *Stuart, stop talking about Vinny!* What are you doing here? What brought you out of your duplex penthouse in New York, on a weekday, a day you could be trading! no less.

STUART. I have some news, Edgar. I'd like you to sit on the couch with me, though.

EDGAR. I'm fine here.

STUART. Please sit on the couch, Edgar. It's big news and I pictured my baby brother sitting next to me, at eye level, not lying on his stoner buddy's floor —

EDGAR. Don't talk about Vinny that way — "stoner," like it's an affliction. Marijuana helps him experience the world in a more vivid and full way; don't be a judger. Some people drink coffee. And I'm staying on the beanbag.

STUART. Okay, win your little battle. You always do. Stay on the beanbag. Are you ready for my news?

EDGAR. No, I don't care.

STUART. Well, I'm gonna tell you: Your big brother has finally settled down.

EDGAR. I don't know what that means, "settled down."

STUART. I'm a husband, man! I got married!

EDGAR. *(Beat.)* Oh. Okay.

STUART. So give me a fucking hug!

EDGAR. Who would marry you?

STUART. You'll meet her, you'll meet her. Her name is Asuncion.

EDGAR. Asuncion … Interesting. She's Latina?

STUART. Yeah, from the Philippines.

EDGAR. That's not — And you married her already? Did you try dating her first?

STUART. No need. No need. It was love at first sight. You'll see.

EDGAR. Wow. Where did you meet her?

STUART. We actually — and this is kind of embarrassing — we met online, on one of those websites. But it's not what it used to be. It's really common now and Sunny was embarrassed too, which was a huge relief.

EDGAR. Hmm. And do you know what part of the Philippines she's from? Because I was in Cambodia.

STUART. I know, Edgar, we all know you were in Cambodia.

EDGAR. I'm just saying, so I can probably relate to her, like maybe better than you.

STUART. We relate to each other just fine, thanks, she's my wife.

EDGAR. Well, the divorce rate is over sixty percent, so statistically —

STUART. Fuck you, I didn't come up here to be insulted by you. I don't have that much time for you to be dicking around here.

EDGAR. But you just got here — it's a three-hour train ride.

STUART. I drove.

EDGAR. You really shouldn't. Foreign oil.

STUART. Shut up. Look, I need a favor.

EDGAR. What?

STUART. I need something kind of big.

EDGAR. Well, I don't have much to give.

STUART. No, you just don't like to give. You're selfish, but you call it depression.

EDGAR. You're maybe the opposite.

STUART. What does that mean?

EDGAR. I wouldn't expect you to know.

STUART. Edgar. I think I'd like some water. *(Edgar moves to the kitchen and turns on the faucet.)*

EDGAR. I let it run so it's cold. Vinny likes the water cold. And I don't have a preference, so I'm used to letting it run. *(Fills the glass, returns to the couch.)* Here. So what's the favor?

STUART. Okay. I — You know you're kind of superior, right?

EDGAR. Thank you.

STUART. No, I mean, you think you're so moral and right, but it's because you do nothing. You know that, right? You're aware of that irony, right?

EDGAR. I don't believe fully in irony.

STUART. You think if you do nothing in the world, you'll feel less guilty, right?

EDGAR. I think if I do nothing bad, I'll feel less guilty. Sure. It's logical.

STUART. Right. But you do do things, Edgar. You do a lot of things. And you can't avoid any of them because you're alive. And often, in the process of living, you fuck some things up.

EDGAR. I can't think of anything that I can't justify. I'm fairly proud.

STUART. You know what happens when you let the water run so it's cold, Edgar?

EDGAR. Vinny likes it cold, and I take quick showers to offset the adverse effects of water usage! I'm very aware!

STUART. You're gracefully missing my point. The world is more complicated than you give it credit for. If you want to sleep on your teacher's floor and never touch your own balls in the shower because your buddy likes his water a little chilled, be my guest. But not everybody's like you.

EDGAR. It's unfortunate.

STUART. I want to be happy, Edgar. I don't want to be like you. And that doesn't make me bad. It makes me practical. *(Composing himself.)* Look, I'm married, now, okay? And I need a favor. I need Asuncion to stay with you. She's downstairs in the car.

EDGAR. Whoa — Stay with us? What?

STUART. It's just for two days.

EDGAR. What the fuck, Stuart, why?

STUART. I can't tell you right now, but we're not in any danger, don't worry.

EDGAR. You can't tell me not to worry!

STUART. Just calm down!

EDGAR. I can't! Now I'm worried! Why do you need her here?

STUART. I can't explain everything —

EDGAR. Explain *something!*

STUART. Stop being so nosey.

EDGAR. I'm sorry; I'm a journalist by trade.

STUART. You're not anything by trade. You don't have a job.

EDGAR. Semantics!

STUART. Just let her hang out up here, okay? I'll be back on Monday. I trust you. It's not a big deal.

EDGAR. I've never even met her!

STUART. She's your sister-in-law. Just do this for me.

EDGAR. I have a roommate. I have Vinny, it's his apartment, I don't even live here! *(We hear Vinny climbing up the stairs.)* Shit, Stuart. He's back! You gotta get out of here.

STUART. Would you grow up?

EDGAR. I'm not supposed to have guests! Shit — ! *(Edgar panics and runs into the bathroom. The door opens and Vinny enters with Asuncion. She is shouldering a duffle bag, carrying a bag from McDonald's and laughing at the punch line of a story.)*

VINNY. So I said if you like mold and no heat, you fucking live there!

ASUNCION. That is fucking hysterical! Stuart, you didn't tell me Vinny was so funny!

STUART. I see you two have already met. Should I be worried?

ASUNCION. No, he's adorable.

VINNY. I'm adorable! You hear that? *(Vinny bear-hugs Stuart.)*

ASUNCION. I feel like every person you introduce me to is funny or something.

VINNY. I'm walking in the house and your wife here — wife! — was just standing there on the porch.

ASUNCION. It was so hot in the car.

VINNY. And I thought, what's a beautiful girl doing outside my apartment!

STUART. *(Laughing.)* Careful, Vinny.

VINNY. You got fucking married?

STUART. Can you believe it?

VINNY. She told me she's gonna stay with us for a few days.

ASUNCION. Only if it's all right, I don't want to be a burden.

VINNY. You could never be a burden; of course it's all right. Is everything okay back home?

STUART. Yeah, we're fine. We're not in any danger, don't worry.

ASUNCION. It's been a nightmare.

STUART. Relax, honey, everything's gonna be fine. I just needed to get her out of the city for a few days.

VINNY. Say no more, say no more. Our *casa* is Sue's *casa*.

STUART. And of course, she wanted to meet Edgar.

VINNY. That should be fun. Where is the little pissant?

STUART. He got scared and ran into the bathroom.

EDGAR. *(Offstage.)* Hi!

VINNY. Come on out, Edgar. I'm not mad. *(Edgar walks out of the bathroom.)*

ASUNCION. Oh my God! You look just like your brother. He's cute, Stuart!

EDGAR. Thank you, Asuncion. It's a pleasure. *Magandang umaga.*

ASUNCION. *Magandang umaga* to you too!

EDGAR. *(To the boys.)* That was a greeting in Tagalog, official language of the Philippines. Roughly translated, it means "beautiful morning." *(To Asuncion.)* I did a little work in Cambodia, I was a journalist — I am a journalist — and I did a little work in Cambodia, so that's why I know … I like to learn one or two phrases in each language. *(Pause.)* I just think your country is so fascinating, Asuncion. Effectively a huge archipelago, made up of Asian people with Spanish names speaking English! The islands, I think there are just over 7,000, is that right?

ASUNCION. Wow.

EDGAR. I know! I always thought the islands were like a perfect metaphor for the disparate effects of colonization. In fact, I wanted to do a piece for *National Geographic* where I try to visit each island without speaking a word of Tagalog, just to see the effects of colonization. I used to do things like that all the time, I used to be inspired.

STUART. Shut the fuck up, Edgar.

VINNY. Yeah, shut the fuck up.

15

EDGAR. I'm being friendly. *(Stuart takes the McDonald's bag from Asuncion.)*

STUART. *(With levity.)* What did I tell you about this shit? It's unhealthy.

ASUNCION. I got the salad, Stuart.

STUART. The dressing.

ASUNCION. It's Newman's Own.

STUART. *(Laughing.)* Isn't she the best? We're trying to do a fast-food-free month kind of thing. Where's the garbage?

EDGAR. Under the sink. *(Stuart takes the McDonald's bag and throws it out.)*

ASUNCION. I was waiting for you for like fifteen minutes, Stuart. I got hungry.

EDGAR. There's a McDonald's around here?

ASUNCION. Down the block. Across from the Shell station.

EDGAR. Is that on Peterson?

ASUNCION. It's like a ten-second walk from here, I don't know.

EDGAR. Huh. A McDonald's. In our neighborhood. I never noticed.

VINNY. Shut the fuck up, Edgar.

EDGAR. What?

VINNY. Don't pretend like you don't know we live next to a McDonald's.

EDGAR. I've truly never noticed it.

VINNY. You're lying. Asuncion, can I get you something to drink?

ASUNCION. No, I'm fine. You guys don't have to worry about me. I'm easy.

STUART. You see? She's the best!

ASUNCION. What do I always say, Stuart?

STUART. Um, I'm not sure which exact thing you're referring to.

ASUNCION. I believe in two things: food and family.

EDGAR. That's a wonderful dogma.

VINNY. The Two F's.

ASUNCION. Yeah, I guess so. "The Two F's."

VINNY. Can I add a third F to the pile?

STUART. Vinny!

VINNY. What? I was gonna suggest friendship! *(Stuart's BlackBerry buzzes.)*

STUART. I got to head out. Thank you, Vinny. Sunny, I will call you later. Thanks, Edgar.

16

EDGAR. Wait a second! Can we all just please sit down for a minute to discuss things.

STUART. I really can't, Edgar. It's Vinny's place and he's cool with it.

EDGAR. Please. This is all moving so fast! I would like to sit down so you can tell me what's going on.

VINNY. You know what's going on. Don't be a child.

EDGAR. You can't just bring over a human and leave!

ASUNCION. You won't even notice me, Edgar.

EDGAR. *(Barks.)* You stay out of this! *(Beat.)* I mean, don't worry about it, we're happy to have you!

VINNY. Edgar, be fucking respectful! They obviously don't want to tell us and I don't want to know anything someone doesn't want me to know. As a rule. You're being ridiculous.

EDGAR. Me? Vinny, you're the one who is so protective of everything in your apartment, who doesn't let me touch anything that's yours. And now she just waltzes in — no offense, Asuncion — and is allowed to stay here?

VINNY. Well, you're creepy. She seems fine.

ASUNCION. Thank you, Vinny.

VINNY. No problem.

EDGAR. I also agree that you're fine, Asuncion. And we could discuss my creepiness later. But right now, could we all just please sit down for five minutes!

VINNY. Edgar, shut up!

STUART. Yeah, shut up!

ASUNCION. Stuart, you can spare five minutes for your brother. Just sit down.

STUART. Fine! We'll sit down.

VINNY. *(Suddenly calm.)* Yeah, we're all family here. Why not? *(They all sit down around the table.)*

STUART. Okay, we're sitting.

EDGAR. Yes, thank you. *(Vinny begins rolling a joint.)* Could you hold off on rolling a joint for five minutes while we discuss this?

VINNY. No.

EDGAR. *(Formal.)* So. Here we are.

STUART. Yeah. We're sitting.

EDGAR. I'm not really sure what else there is to discuss.

STUART. Okay. *(They all stand back up. Stuart shakes their hands.)* Men. I will speak to you. Sunny, I love you to peaches!

ASUNCION. I love you to peaches! *(Kissing Stuart.)*

VINNY. Adorable. *(Stuart exits the apartment. Vinny continues rolling the joint. Edgar and Asuncion stare at each other.)*

EDGAR. No one's going to hurt you.

ASUNCION. Thanks! It's so great to finally meet you.

EDGAR. Would you like me to hug you?

ASUNCION. Um, definitely not. I'm totally sticky from the car ride.

VINNY. *(Without looking up.)* Eww.

EDGAR. I completely understand. And I'm sorry to have been so forward.

ASUNCION. No problem. Can I actually take a shower?

EDGAR. Of course! Do you need soaps?

ASUNCION. No, I have soap. Where's the bathroom?

EDGAR. In there! Have a nice shower, Asuncion! *(Asuncion exits into the bathroom and we hear the shower turn on. Vinny casually lights up his joint.)* We gotta get her out of here!

VINNY. What?

EDGAR. Or maybe we should get out of here and call the police.

VINNY. What the hell are you talking about?

EDGAR. Okay, Vinny, I think — and just hear me out here — but I think she might be a sex slave.

VINNY. Excuse me?

EDGAR. It's not clear to you?

VINNY. What's not clear?

EDGAR. All the clues!

VINNY. Dude, what clues?

EDGAR. She is from the Philippines, Vinny! You're practically born into the sex trade there if you're not from fucking white European colonial descent.

VINNY. I'm sure there are women from the Philippines who aren't sex slaves.

EDGAR. Yeah? Name one! He's probably hiding her out here! Homeland Security is probably on to them and that's why he wouldn't tell us what's going on! It's all starting to gel.

VINNY. Calm down! What did he tell you? Did he say where they met?

EDGAR. Yes! On the internet! And I've been to these websites, for my work. You go online, there are thousands of pictures of young girls. Remember I wrote that article, "The Meat Market of Europe" about Ukraine? Well, the Philippines is the same thing, but with Asians.

18

VINNY. I don't think Stuart would do that.

EDGAR. Stuart is exactly the kind of guy who does shit like this. He lost his virginity to a prostitute in Red Bank.

VINNY. He did?

EDGAR. Yes, on prom night.

VINNY. I didn't know that. Either way, you're an idiot. Look, if you think she's a sex worker, just ask her.

EDGAR. No! You can't ask a victim about their oppressor. They're brainwashed to worship them and lie. We have to be very gentle with her. And when Stuart returns on Monday, we hide Asuncion, call the police from the bathroom and have Stuart arrested.

VINNY. So she can stay until Monday?

EDGAR. Yes, until I sort out what to do.

VINNY. Good, she's kind of hot.

EDGAR. Vinny! Don't say that! Don't sexualize her!

VINNY. Why not? She is.

EDGAR. She's not for that kind of consumption. She's to be pitied! She's a victim, she's a sex slave victim!

VINNY. Well, if she is, it's because she's hot.

EDGAR. Vinny!

VINNY. Don't feel so guilty, Edgar. Women like her, if she is a sex worker — and don't say slaves — they think of sex differently. They've been trained to do it to please the man rather than receive pleasure themselves, so it's thought of like a service, rather than as recreation.

EDGAR. No. Sex should be a mutually enjoyable experience. If it has to be had.

VINNY. So should skiing. Which you hate. But when your fat little girlfriend wanted to go skiing last year, you went with her, because you were fucking her and it was worth it. Sometimes two people do things that one of them enjoys more.

EDGAR. Huh. That's not a bad point.

VINNY. Fuck you, don't condescend.

EDGAR. Sorry.

VINNY. This is interesting. Let's travel down this garden path for a minute. A sex worker might be in our house. And a sex worker's duty is to please the man of the house. Which, in this case, is so obviously me. In fact, I think I may take her skiing.

EDGAR. Vinny! She's my brother's wife!

VINNY. She's staying in my apartment. *Quid pro quo.*

EDGAR. Vinny, please …

VINNY. You may want to hit the slopes yourself, young Eddie!

EDGAR. This is absurd! I can't tell if you're joking!

VINNY. Me neither.

EDGAR. She's my sister!

VINNY. She's not your sister! And you haven't had sex for a year. It's not healthy, Edgar.

EDGAR. Stop talking like this, it's disgusting. *(Intimately.)* It's been more than a year. And I haven't masturbated in three months.

VINNY. Jesus, Edgar! Don't tell me that!

EDGAR. The last time I masturbated, I did it for five hours. Five hours, one ejaculation. I hated myself for a whole week after that. I couldn't look in a mirror. I couldn't look at my naked body. I dressed at night in the dark and slept in my clothes and wore them the next day so I wouldn't ever see me. And my penis was smaller than ever. It was like it was dried and bagged. Like NASA ice cream or a shriveled apricot that occasionally pissed.

VINNY. *(Gently.)* You're unhealthy, buddy.

EDGAR. I used to be inspired.

VINNY. *(Laughing.)* You should cure yourself by having sex with your sister, Edgar. *(Edgar laughs too.)* Actually, what you should do, Edgar, what you should do — You should write a story about her.

EDGAR. Huh …

VINNY. While she's here. You should write a story about her, about her plight. A personal account of Asuncion, an orphan child born on the streets of Calcutta — or wherever she's from, you can work out those details on your own — and hidden in the hull of a steamer, gnawing on the fallen breadcrumbs from her master's supper, and traversing the seven seas just to marry your dumb brother.

EDGAR. That's actually a great idea.

VINNY. You could be published!

EDGAR. You think?

VINNY. And then pay me some rent.

EDGAR. *The Nation* would take something like this —

VINNY. Even *Vanity Fair* —

EDGAR. I could win a Pulitzer!

VINNY. I don't think you'll win a Pulitzer.

EDGAR. Well, you said *Vanity Fair*, so I was just going along with the dream —

VINNY. It's good to have dreams, Edgar.

EDGAR. But you can't tell her what I'm doing.

VINNY. Don't tell me what to do.

EDGAR. Oh right, sorry.

VINNY. And don't apologize.

EDGAR. Okay, sor — Okay. I could call it "A Woman In The Shadows." No, no … "Out from the Shadows."

VINNY. What about … "The Pacific Rim-Job."

EDGAR. That's good — that's funny. What about "Stopped Traffick"?

VINNY. "The Great Barrier Queef"!

EDGAR. I'm going to write something so great, Vinny. I'm going to save her! *(We hear the shower turn off. The bathroom door opens and Asuncion exits in Vinny's robe.)*

ASUNCION. I found this robe, I hope it's okay.

VINNY. Of course! It's mine, but you can keep it.

EDGAR. Yeah, no problem! *(Asuncion walks to the garbage can, opens it and pulls out her McDonald's bag, placing it on the table. Then she casually moves to the couch, grabs her duffle bag and exits into the bathroom. Edgar runs to his shelf and digs through his clothes, finding a spiral notebook and pen.)*

VINNY. What the hell are you doing? Put that away! *(Edgar quickly hides the notebook as Asuncion emerges from the bathroom.)*

ASUNCION. Okay, I'm clean now, Edgar, I can give you that hug!

EDGAR. Oh! I didn't think you were unclean before. But we don't have to hug; there's no pressure.

VINNY. I'll take that hug! Come here! *(Vinny grabs Asuncion and squeezes her.)* That felt good.

ASUNCION. I'm glad. Your turn, Mr. Edgar.

EDGAR. Okay, sure! You really don't need to do this.

ASUNCION. Please! It's what I do. *(Edgar hugs Asuncion while desperately trying to keep his pelvis away from her. She looks at him tenderly and strokes his face.)* Stuart's little brother.

EDGAR. Thank you. Thank you, Asuncion.

VINNY. Yes. Thank you. For all that you've done. And all that you're going to do. *(Blackout.)*

Scene 3

The next day.

Edgar sits on the couch, dressed impeccably and holding his notepad.

Asuncion enters and walks into the kitchen, where she fills a pot with water and lights it on the stove. She then takes a mug from the cabinet and a bag of tea from her purse.

EDGAR. *Umaga*, Asuncion.
ASUNCION. Ah! Shit! *(She has spilled water on the floor.)* Sorry, Edgar, I didn't see you there.
EDGAR. I know. *(Asuncion begins cleaning the water from the floor.)* I'm glad we can finally get some face time, just the two of us, and I want to say that I'm sorry for my hesitant behavior in taking you in yesterday.
ASUNCION. No, I totally get it, Edgar. We're cool. I hate making weird decisions.
EDGAR. I'm occasionally indecisive, but once I make a decision I stick with it all the way!
ASUNCION. Oh, I thought this was Vinny's place.
EDGAR. Well, we approved the decision equally. And I'm related to you, so that's how it's equal. Now that's settled. The fine print and such. So, I'm interested in hearing about your very fascinating life.
ASUNCION. You too.
EDGAR. Oh, me? I'm just a big bowl of boring.
ASUNCION. Something tells me that's not exactly true, Edgar.
EDGAR. You're right. I sell myself too short. But I'd like to start with you. Come to the couch. You could bring the tea. I'm sure it's ready.
ASUNCION. Did you want a cup too? I brought some special tea that they only sell at this tiny Filipina shop in the city.
EDGAR. No thanks. I don't like tea.
ASUNCION. Oh, sorry.

EDGAR. No problem! *(Asuncion pours herself a mug and brings it to the couch.)* So, how long have you been in this country, Asuncion?

ASUNCION. Like two years this September.

EDGAR. Interesting. What brought you over here?

ASUNCION. You mean like, how did I get here?

EDGAR. We don't have to get into that stuff right away. But, why did you want to come here?

ASUNCION. Well, my mother died and I kind of just got really depressed, you know? I started doing dumb things and hanging out with some bad people. So my father thought a change of environment would be good for me.

EDGAR. Hmm. Well, we all have our demons. You should try to remember that. And it may be hard to believe, but even I've struggled with my own troubles.

ASUNCION. Really, like what?

EDGAR. Some things I've seen. Some hardships. I actually wrote a blog post about some things I've witnessed in your neck of the woods, Cambodia. Do you mind if I share it with you?

ASUNCION. I'm from the Philippines.

EDGAR. Let me get it. *(Edgar rifles through his stuff, pulls out a piece of paper.)* I submitted this to *The Nation* and got a wonderful response, but they couldn't print it, I assume because they've become a little corporate. Do you mind if I read you the whole thing?

ASUNCION. Please do.

EDGAR. Thank you. *(Clears his throat, reads.)* "Western hotels line the sandy streets of Cambodia like proverbial oases in the desert. But these are not oases. For do oases employ dozens of workers at fifty cents an hour? Do oases suck the resources of a single city, depriving the indigenous residents of electricity? No. Oases are figments of an imagination under extreme duress. And therefore oases are not real. What are real, though, are the problems facing Siem Reap, a miserable city in Cambodia. Siem Reap was cursed with the architectural wonder Angkor Wat and is condemned to pillage by tourists twelve months a year, which means all year. Tourists like hotels and they are lining the sandy streets of Siem Reap like patients lining up for AIDS treatment at the local hospital, which is another problem facing Cambodia. (Look for it in my next post!) I've attached a picture of me in front of one of the monstrosity Hilton hotel chains."

ASUNCION. *(Pause.)* Is that the ending?

EDGAR. Yeah.

ASUNCION. Where's the picture?

EDGAR. What picture?

ASUNCION. In front of the nice hotel.

EDGAR. Oh, it's on my site, on my website, which I don't have anymore.

ASUNCION. Oh, that sucks.

EDGAR. I _____ best post. I would ___ ___ it better if I really _____ _____ e detracts from an

EDGAR. You really tʜ.... Because I so often receive feedback that indicates otherwise.

ASUNCION. Well, I think you're great.

EDGAR. *(Very moved.)* You. You are a breath of fresh air, Asuncion! You are a wonderful human being. You are … you are better than America. You should go back home — I mean I'm glad you're here, I really am — but you're better than us. I really have to apologize for our imperialism and arrogance. I'm embarrassed for my country.

ASUNCION. Don't apologize, Edgar, I love America.

EDGAR. Interesting! What do you love about it?

ASUNCION. I love everything that's American! Why do you think I stayed here for so long?

EDGAR. This is scintillating!

ASUNCION. I think of it like a pop song, you know? In a pop song, it's only the good stuff. In a long boring song, like Beethoven or something, there's only a few good parts, and the songs are like ten minutes long. But in a pop song, it's like they took out the best three minutes of the Beethoven and put it into one song. And that's how I think of America, you know? It's like they took the best things from the rest of the world and made a pop song nation.

EDGAR. A pop song nation! Fascinating!

ASUNCION. Do you think I could put some music on?

EDGAR. Sure, of course! We'll do the music. But not now. Later! Later for music. I feel like I'm kind of on a roll, don't you?

ASUNCION. I guess so.

EDGAR. Me too. Can I pick your brain?

ASUNCION. What do you mean?

EDGAR. I'm sorry, I just really respect your perspective. Do you mind if I ask you some questions and record your responses?

ASUNCION. Um … I guess it's okay. It's a little weird.

EDGAR. No, I don't think it's weird at all, I think you're great. *(Edgar runs to his shelf and finds a small tape recorder.)* Okay, interview Saturday, May 19th with Asuncion — wait, did you take my brother's last name when you got married?

ASUNCION. Yeah, of course.

EDGAR. Okay, interview Saturday May 19th, 10 A.M., with Asuncion Hirschhorn. Asuncion, I want to know everything you think — everything about the world — the world through your eyes!

ASUNCION. Okay. *(Pause.)* Well, I guess I feel like there are two different kinds of people, you know? And I'm not talking God or anything, but I feel like some people are good, even though maybe they get into trouble, and some people are bad, even though they're the ones everyone thinks is good. Like I have this cousin Rafael who acts like he's this great guy, but he really should be in prison, you know?

EDGAR. Maybe I should steer the questions a little more directly. I was kind of hoping to know your take on Cambodia.

ASUNCION. Okay, but you know I'm not from Cambodia, right? I'm from the Philippines.

EDGAR. Exactly! I hate how everybody just lumps every country that's not America into one thing! So I would like to know your take on post-Vietnam Cambodia. Because I kind of had an interesting experience there — I met a guy who I really liked. His name was Bon-Sun.

ASUNCION. I don't know him.

EDGAR. No, I know, I'm just telling you about him.

ASUNCION. Oh, sorry.

EDGAR. Don't be sorry. Don't ever. Not with me. So Bon-Sun invites me to this little bar, which was owned by an Australian guy so he thought I would like it which is totally sweet but in a kind of reverse-racist way. And he gets pretty drunk and starts talking about, Pol Pot. And I'm ecstatic, because that's really all I want to talk about but everyone's so sensitive over there, so it doesn't come up that much. So I keep my mouth shut and just listen to him and he starts going off about how great Pol Pot is. And I'm shocked, of course. Like who is this guy? Anyway, my point, I guess, not that we all need points, I don't believe in always having to make a point, Asuncion, but what I'm kind of wondering is what you think about Pol Pot.

ASUNCION. Pol Pot?

EDGAR. *(Edge of seat.)* Pol Pot.

ASUNCION. I know he was in Cambodia.

EDGAR. Yes...?

ASUNCION. And I think he was really bad, you know?

EDGAR. Fascinating! You think he was bad, and Bon-Sun thought he saved Southeast Asia from Western imperialism!

ASUNCION. And I think he killed a lot of people, too.

EDGAR. Yes! That's so interesting to hear you say that! Because a lot of people think Kang Kek Lew was mainly responsible for the genocide. You know?

ASUNCION. Well, I guess it could've been him, too.

EDGAR. Exactly! And I have to remember to keep that in mind. Because I feel like Americans tend to demonize one person for an entire genocide. And Bon-Sun wasn't doing that, which was so smart. Because after I left Bon-Sun, after I departed Cambodia, I realized I'm this fucking American, you know? I could be from fucking Paraguay or Azerbaijan and I would never think twice about my own opinion, you know? It's this very American thing, this false superior perspective!

ASUNCION. You're so smart, Edgar. Just like your brother.

EDGAR. Life lessons, Asuncion! Every day, I try to learn something new. Sometimes two things! Hey Asuncion, are you hungry?

ASUNCION. Kind of. But I could wait ...

EDGAR. Of course you can wait, that's just me thinking like an American again! "Everything has to be here immediately! Roar!" I'm gonna pick up some bagels. Does that sound good?

ASUNCION. Sure.

EDGAR. Great. Vinny should be up soon. He likes it when he wakes up to hot bagels. And I like it when he likes things. *(Edgar grabs his bicycle and opens the door.)* I'm really happy you're here, Asuncion.

ASUNCION. Thank you, Edgar.

EDGAR. And I'm happy you're my sister-in-law.

ASUNCION. Thank you, Edgar.

EDGAR. I'm happy, Asuncion! I'm actually happy! *(Edgar exits with his bike. Asuncion finishes her tea and takes the cup to the sink. She takes an iPod out of her purse and plugs it into the stereo. She turns it on and her pop music blares loudly.)*

ASUNCION. Shit shit shit! *(She lowers the volume on the stereo, grabs her cell from her purse and dials.)* Hey, it's me. Just talk to me for a minute. Okay. I miss you too. Yeah, they're fine, they're sweet. On the floor. Vinny's room. Did you speak to anyone yet? What? Why?! Okay, I'll figure something out. I'll call you there later. I love you, too. *(Asuncion hangs up the phone anxiously and walks to her purse, as Vinny enters, having just woken up.)* Hey Vinny.

VINNY. You woke me up, Asuncion. The stereo woke me up. The volume you selected.

ASUNCION. Sorry, I'll turn it off.

VINNY. No, don't apologize. Turn it up! We should listen to whatever it is that you like. *(Vinny turns the music up. Asuncion shouts over the loud music.)*

ASUNCION. Listen, Vinny, I just spoke to Stuart and —

VINNY. You're going to have to talk louder, sweetheart! The music's overpowering your voice. *(Asuncion walks to the stereo and turns it down.)* That's better.

ASUNCION. I said that I just spoke to Stuart and he told me that he can't get me until late next week.

VINNY. Well, that's no problem. More for us. Is everything all right?

ASUNCION. Yeah, it's fine. I saw a Holiday Inn down the road, I'll just pack my things and get out of your hair.

VINNY. You don't have to go anywhere. Women stay over here all the time. Edgar's a woman and he's been here for years.

ASUNCION. Are you sure?

VINNY. Always.

ASUNCION. Awesome! To be honest, I'm a little freaked out by hotels.

VINNY. Thank you for your honesty. Now. Where is Edgar? Is he pooping?

ASUNCION. No, he went to get bagels.

VINNY. Good, good. Did you two have a nice chat?

ASUNCION. Yeah. He's sweet.

VINNY. He didn't get too personal, did he?

ASUNCION. No. He knows so much about history.

VINNY. He does know so much about history. If it ever gets weird, you let me know, okay? I'm here for you.

ASUNCION. What do you mean?

VINNY. Did you sleep well?

ASUNCION. The floor was a little hard.

VINNY. Was it? I'll call the super. But in the meantime, you could take my bed.

ASUNCION. Really? Thank you!

VINNY. But I might be there, too.

ASUNCION. You're crazy, Vinny.

VINNY. *(Oddly shouts.)* NO, YOU ARE!

ASUNCION. You know, Mr. Vinny, Stuart warned me all about you.

VINNY. Only nice things, I hope.

ASUNCION. How he used to take you out when he would come visit Edgar. And the two of you would chase girls across campus.

VINNY. They are still on the run, Asuncion. *(Vinny walks into the bathroom and leaves the door open as he pisses.)* Asuncion.

ASUNCION. Yeah?

VINNY. No, I'm just saying your name.

ASUNCION. Oh, sorry.

VINNY. Don't say sorry. "Asuncion." It's a beautiful name.

ASUNCION. Thanks!

VINNY. I love the way it just rolls off my tongue.

ASUNCION. My name is about Mary. Asuncion. My dad was like a religious nut. And I was like, "Dad, if you want me to have a normal childhood, give me like a freaking normal name." You know?

VINNY. *(Exits the bathroom.)* Your dad sounds like an idiot. It means assumption. *(Vinny begins rolling his morning joint.)* Quieres mi churro?

ASUNCION. What?

VINNY. *Queires un poco heirba?*

ASUNCION. What?

VINNY. *Hablas español?* Do you not speak Spanish?

ASUNCION. I speak Tagalog.

VINNY. But your name … Fuck, even I speak Spanish. You're in America now, Asuncion, you're going to have to learn some Spanish. What I said was, would you like to partake? *(Vinny lights the joint.)*

ASUNCION. I don't think that's a good idea.

VINNY. *(Sing-song.)* I don't either.

ASUNCION. Well, maybe just one little puff.

VINNY. There she is.

ASUNCION. But don't tell Stuart.

VINNY. Who's Stuart?

ASUNCION. *Ay' bastos. (They giggle together, getting closer on the couch. She takes a hit and coughs.)* It's been a while.

VINNY. Welcome back. You know, Edgar's been spreading rumors about you. All around the house.

ASUNCION. Rumors? What did he say?

VINNY. Oh, nothing. Just stories about your life. Your past. Your present. Are they true?

ASUNCION. I feel like Edgar kind of talks a lot. Do you know what I mean?

VINNY. I do know what you mean. The boy needs a lot of love. We all do. Look, I get it, everyone does what they need to do. I think it's a good thing actually. And you could stay here as long as you want. As long as you need. As it takes.

ASUNCION. Thanks! Do you mind if I put my music up?

VINNY. Of course not. You don't have to ask me that.

ASUNCION. Okay, good. 'Cause Edgar didn't want me to play it.

VINNY. Well, I'm not Edgar.

ASUNCION. I can see that. *(She turns up her pop music.)* Do you want to see my dance?

VINNY. Your dance?

ASUNCION. You have to promise not to laugh though, okay?

VINNY. Yes, ma'am! *(Asuncion begins doing a choreographed dance to the song.)* I want you to never stop doing that dance, ever.

ASUNCION. Shh. I have to focus. Watch this! *(She does a little move.)*

VINNY. Yeah! I like it. I like your music, Asuncion! I like this beat! It's tribal! *(Vinny grabs his djembe and begins playing in time with the music.)*

ASUNCION. Do you want me to teach you the moves?

VINNY. Dancing's not meant to be taught. It's a feeling. The actual steps are just clumsy physical manifestations.

ASUNCION. You're crazy, Vinny.

VINNY. You have no idea. *(They begin dancing closer, Asuncion still doing her moves, Vinny gyrating wildly.)*

ASUNCION. I feel like Stuart and I never dance anymore!

VINNY. I feel like Edgar and I never dance anymore, either! A man needs to move, you know?

ASUNCION. So does a woman!

VINNY. We're from the same tribe, Asuncion. I'm an Africanist. Do you know what that means?

ASUNCION. Does it mean you dance like a crazy person?

VINNY. Close. It means I believe in Africa. And as an Africanist,

I get to play by different rules. We both do. *(Vinny throws the Pan-African flag around his back and dramatically bangs the djembe.)* Did you know that in the ancient Patchaka tribe, it was customary for the weakest warrior to be sent out, hunting for antelopes or water-fowls or bagels? But while the young tribesman was out, the chief would bed the most fertile member of the tribe.

ASUNCION. That's not funny, Vinny.

VINNY. In Africa, they think it's hysterical. Do you wanna join the tribe? *(Vinny grabs Asuncion's cell phone from the table.)*

ASUNCION. Who are you calling? *(He begins chanting into her cell phone.)*

VINNY. I'm calling the tribe. *(Chants into phone.)* Oh, they want to speak to you! Say hi to the tribe!

ASUNCION. Hey, tribe! What's up? *(They crack up laughing, Vinny chanting into the phone. Asuncion grabs the end of Vinny's flag and he pulls her into him. They dance together. The music swells, the lights begin to fade and, in near darkness, Edgar walks in shouldering his bicycle, which has been mangled. His face is, again, dripping with blood.)*

VINNY. You are a breath of fresh air, Asuncion! *(Blackout.)*

End of Act One

ACT TWO

Scene 1

One week later.

The world map has been taken down from the center of the room revealing a large open window, which looks out onto Binghamton.

The house is spotless. Light streams in. The sink is empty and the plates are stacked high to dry.

Edgar is on the floor, making notes on scrap paper and Post-It notes.

Edgar hears Vinny and Asuncion walking up the stairs and begins frantically cleaning up his note scraps. Vinny and Asuncion enter.

ASUNCION. Edgar, we're back!
VINNY. Yes, and we come bearing bagels!
ASUNCION. Your personal favorite, vegetable cream cheese on an everything.
EDGAR. Perfect, perfect.
ASUNCION. Vinny of course got whole wheat and plain cream cheese. Boring Vinny!
EDGAR. Yeah, boring!
ASUNCION. Big bowl of boring Vinny!
VINNY. Oh yeah? Tell him what you got, Sunny.
ASUNCION. Chopped liver on a chocolate chip bagel. So what?
EDGAR. Asuncion, that's disgusting!
ASUNCION. I like to try new things.
VINNY. I know that's the truth.
ASUNCION. Shut up, Vinny.

VINNY. What? It's a compliment! *(Edgar brings three plates from the counter.)*

EDGAR. Did you notice the house?

VINNY. What about it?

EDGAR. It's clean, it's spotless.

ASUNCION. I noticed, Edgar. It looks beautiful.

VINNY. *(Looks around.)* It's not a total fucking disaster, I'll give you that.

EDGAR. And the dishes are washed; I can actually see the bottom of the sink for the first time since I moved in. *(Beat, jokey.)* It's silver, in case you're wondering.

VINNY. *(Suddenly bitter.)* Well, you moved in a long time ago.

EDGAR. I was just making a joke, Jesus.

VINNY. There's a time when joking stops.

EDGAR. Vinny …

ASUNCION. *(Trying to diffuse tension.)* Hey, Vinny, tell Edgar about the OJ woman.

VINNY. You tell him. I'm eating.

ASUNCION. You do the voice so good, though!

EDGAR. What OJ woman?

ASUNCION. Okay, there was this woman in front of us on line. And she was kind of like this big black woman, and she kept saying, *(A dramatic voice.)* "I want some OJ! I want some OJ!" I can't do the voice, Vinny, you do it!

VINNY. *(Lackluster.)* Gimme some fucking OJ!

ASUNCION. *(Laughing hysterically.)* Do it again better!

VINNY. *(Bigger.)* I want some OJ!

ASUNCION. Edgar, isn't that fucking hysterical?

EDGAR. Maybe. I mean the voice is a little offensive but —

ASUNCION. Do it again, Vinny!

VINNY. I want some FUCKIN' OJ!

ASUNCION. Edgar, isn't that just the funniest thing you ever did hear?

EDGAR. Well, maybe. I guess you had to be there.

ASUNCION. I don't know, maybe. You're crazy, Vinny. *(Asuncion flips on the stereo.)* So do you guys care what we listen to?

EDGAR. Actually, yes. I would like to listen to nothing.

VINNY. And I would like to listen to some fucking OJ!

EDGAR. Please, Asuncion, can we just keep it off for breakfast? We have bagels. We should just enjoy each other's company.

ASUNCION. Okay. I could enjoy both, but okay. *(Vinny crosses to the stereo and flips it back on.)*

VINNY. What do you want to listen to, Sunny?

ASUNCION. I think Edgar wants to just enjoy each other and I think that's a nice idea.

VINNY. Okay, we'll keep it off, but you better fucking enjoy me, Edgar.

EDGAR. I will. *(They resume eating.)* You see? Isn't this nice, just sitting around eating, quietly? Listening to the sounds of nature. *(We hear a motorcycle zoom past the house.)* How's the bagel, Asuncion? Is it totally disgusting?

VINNY. Jesus, Edgar! Why the fuck are you always so negative?

EDGAR. I'm not being negative! We were just joking before about the bagel, so —

VINNY. If we're not gonna listen to her music, at least let us enjoy our bounty.

ASUNCION. Actually, this is pretty disgusting.

EDGAR. See?

VINNY. I told you, Sunny — it's a vile combination. You gotta listen to me.

ASUNCION. I know, I know.

VINNY. Do you want to trade?

ASUNCION. No, I break it, I get to buy it!

VINNY. Not if you don't like it. I really don't mind.

EDGAR. Yeah, me neither, you could have mine, it's delicious.

ASUNCION. Guys! I'm fine! It's okay.

EDGAR. Just let me know.

VINNY. Yo, she said she's fine.

EDGAR. Cool. *(Asuncion spits out her bite of bagel and wraps it up. She brings it to the garbage.)*

VINNY. What's wrong?

ASUNCION. Nothing, I'm just not that hungry. I think I'm actually gonna jump into a shower.

EDGAR. Really? We just sat down.

ASUNCION. I haven't showered yet today. Really, I'm fine. I'll be out in a minute.

EDGAR. Okay.

VINNY. Take your time in there! You smell like shit!

ASUNCION. I want some OJ!

VINNY. Give me my motherfucking OJ! *(Asuncion exits into the*

bathroom, laughing. Edgar runs to the garbage and peeks in.)
EDGAR. I think she threw away the whole thing.
VINNY. She said it was disgusting. *(Edgar grabs a pen and begins writing on a napkin.)* What are you writing?
EDGAR. The OJ thing.
VINNY. Why?
EDGAR. I think it's kind of important, socio-politically, race relations — I'm documenting everything and, Vinny, I can't tell you how amazingly this is coming! I'm about to finish the first part. I imagine it will be a triptych.
VINNY. A triptych?
EDGAR. Yeah, that's a Greco-Roman writing tablet—
VINNY. I know what a fucking triptych is.
EDGAR. *(Undaunted.)* Awesome, me too! She is totally fascinating. The way that she's always so agreeable. The three showers a day thing, which seems excessive but makes sense, the need to cleanse, the need to restore. I actually think she may be bulimic; she seems to shower after eating — case in point. Do you think she's bulimic? *(Vinny doesn't answer.)* But she seems healthy. Do bulimics absorb nutrition from food before they puke? I don't know. I'm thinking it will be a multi-part expose. I'm calling her Sarah for anonymity's sake.
VINNY. Sarah.
EDGAR. I haven't asked her about any sexual experiences yet, it feels gauche at this point, but I'm working up to it, developing a trust.
VINNY. *(Disgusted.)* She seems to really feel comfortable with you.
EDGAR. And how do you like the title, "Sarah's Story: From the Slums of the Philippines to the Slums of Humanity"?
VINNY. I think it's weird.
EDGAR. Yeah, I don't think I'll keep it. But check this out. Since she's been here, I've documented everything she's done and you know how she's always biting her nails?
VINNY. No.
EDGAR. Really? She always does that. Anyway, I've noticed that she only bites her right hand during the day, but at night she switches to the left hand. It could just be coincidental, that's why I wish I had more time with her, but I'm getting some incredible field notes.
VINNY. Don't say field notes.
EDGAR. I feel inspired, I actually like waking up in the morning.

(Finds a scrap.) Oh! This one's priceless. I asked her who her personal heroes were? She could name anyone in the history of man — Gandhi, Mother Theresa, Chomsky, anyone! And guess who she says? Guess who she fucking says?!

VINNY. I don't know, man.

EDGAR. Mariah Carey! Fucking Mariah Carey. I didn't even know who that was. Turns out she's a fucking pop singer!

VINNY. Everybody knows who Mariah Carey is, Edgar, don't pretend you don't know about pop culture.

EDGAR. Oh, come on. You don't think that's funny?

VINNY. No, and frankly I think it's offensive that you've spent the last week writing down everything she says and does. "Nothing is more dangerous than sincere ignorance."

EDGAR. Malcolm X?

VINNY. MLK, dude.

EDGAR. I don't know why you're so mad. I'm just trying to write an article about the sex trade! And it was your idea!

VINNY. But you're not. You're just writing about a woman who bites her nails. And then criticizing her behind her back. It's insulting.

EDGAR. Vinny!

VINNY. You still think she's a sex worker?

EDGAR. What do you mean?

VINNY. I mean she's been here for a week. Have you actually asked her what it is that she does?

EDGAR. Not in so many words, but I think it's pretty clear.

VINNY. If you're so curious, I think you should just ask her about her years as a prostitute. I'll help you out. Hey, Asuncion!

EDGAR. Vinny! No! It's way too soon; it's way too soon for my subject — for Asuncion. What about what you're doing? Taking advantage of her like that.

VINNY. Like what?

EDGAR. Vinny, please. I haven't said anything because I thought you might kick her out.

VINNY. Said anything about what? What the hell are you talking about?

EDGAR. The way you're — that you're — She's my brother's wife, Vinny!

VINNY. Yeah...?

EDGAR. And you're — you're f-fucking her.

35

VINNY. Excuse me?

EDGAR. I shouldn't have said anything.

VINNY. Yeah, maybe not.

EDGAR. It's not my business, maybe.

VINNY. You should think before you speak.

EDGAR. I'm perhaps more uncomfortable with sex than average, so I shouldn't pry.

VINNY. Edgar!

EDGAR. Yes?

VINNY. I never fucked her.

EDGAR. *(Beat.)* You didn't?

VINNY. No! What do you think I am? We're just hanging out. She's cool.

EDGAR. But I thought —

VINNY. I flirt, but that's just like what I fucking do, you know? I tease. But I'm not fucking her. We just get along.

EDGAR. Oh. What do you guys talk about?

VINNY. Nothing. Anything. Whatever. She's funny.

EDGAR. She's funny?!

VINNY. Yes. Actually.

EDGAR. Like witty? Or more observational-type humor?

VINNY. I don't know, she's just chill, she's just fun to have around.

EDGAR. I can be chill.

VINNY. No, you can't.

EDGAR. I'm chill right now!

VINNY. No, and you never have been.

EDGAR. Well, I'm fun!

VINNY. Nope.

EDGAR. No?

VINNY. Never.

EDGAR. I'm not fun? I'm not fun!? I'm fun! I'm so much fun! Last week, last week, I bought that six-pack of soy chocolate pudding! And I ate three of them in one night. That very same night.

VINNY. That's not fun, that's gluttonous!

EDGAR. No! It's not gluttonous because I'm so thin, so it's fun! It's fun! Or what about that time you wanted to start doing graffiti and I came up with the word to write!?

VINNY. You wanted me to write, "Madam I'm Adam."

EDGAR. And other palindromes! I think it would be funny on the side of a bus — "Ah, Satan sees Natasha" or "Do geese see

God?" on the side of a mailbox or an ice cream truck. It's funny!

VINNY. No, it's not.

EDGAR. Well, it's witty, it's subversive, it's something. It is!

VINNY. No it's not. You're not subversive, you're not whimsical, you're definitely not chill. And, no, Edgar, you are not fun. And you have never been fun.

EDGAR. I'm sorry.

VINNY. Don't say sorry.

EDGAR. Okay. *(Pause.)* Do you like me at all? *(Pause.)* Do you like anything about me? *(Vinny stares ahead. We hear the shower turn off. Asuncion enters from the bathroom in a robe.)*

ASUNCION. Where's my motherfuckin' OJ at?!

VINNY. I got your OJ right here, girl! *(Hits his lap.)*

ASUNCION. It gots pulp?

VINNY. You bet your ass it gots pulp!

EDGAR. Okay, guys, really it's starting to get —

ASUNCION. Is the pulp thick?

VINNY. Thick as a brick!

EDGAR. Guys, please, it's a —

ASUNCION. Oh yeah? You think I can handle it?

EDGAR. *(Exploding.)* Would both of you shut the fuck up about the fucking orange juice?!

ASUNCION. *(Beat.)* Whoa.

EDGAR. *(Sober.)* Sorry, I'm a little — I just — I thought you might be cold just in Vinny's robe. You should maybe go change?

ASUNCION. Think I'll do that. *(Asuncion begins to cross off to the bedroom.)*

VINNY. *(Quietly.)* Gimme some OJ.

ASUNCION. *(Chokes back a laugh.)* Vinny, shut up … *(Asuncion exits into the bedroom.)*

EDGAR. Thank you for turning me into the bad guy.

VINNY. You do that yourself.

EDGAR. Well, maybe you serve as a reflection.

VINNY. Did you write down the color of her robe?

EDGAR. Shut up.

VINNY. Did you time her shower?

EDGAR. Shh! Vinny! She's right in the bedroom! *(Asuncion reenters, having changed.)*

ASUNCION. Yo, yo, boring little Vinny, we gonna drop?

VINNY. Hell, yes.

ASUNCION. You gots the goods?

VINNY. You knows it.

EDGAR. What's happening?

ASUNCION. You have enough? 'Cuz I need two.

VINNY. I picked up, like, fifteen after class.

ASUNCION. From Jeremiah?

VINNY. No, Shaksey.

ASUNCION. *(Excited.)* Oh shit!

EDGAR. Hello! What's going on here?

ASUNCION. I thought Jeremiah told you — I thought he promised you —

EDGAR. What are you guys doing? Who's Shaksey?

VINNY. Shaksey's my dealer.

ASUNCION. Shaksey's a fucking mental patient!

EDGAR. Your dealer? Wait — You both know a person named Shaksey?

ASUNCION. Yeah, he's retarded — Vinny and I are gonna drop tonight.

EDGAR. Drop what? What does that mean?

VINNY. Edgar don't know the lingo.

ASUNCION. Oh, sorry, Edgar — we're going to be swallowing tabs of LSD acid. That is if Vinny agrees not to try on every one of my skirts again.

VINNY. I agree, *señorita.*

EDGAR. Again?

VINNY. Yeah, Wednesday, we tripped Wednesday as well.

EDGAR. Wednesday? I was here Wednesday.

VINNY. Yeah, you went to sleep.

ASUNCION. We didn't want to wake you up.

EDGAR. Why? I'm a night owl usually.

ASUNCION. Sorry, I wish I knew, I would have told you.

VINNY. He wouldn't have done it anyway.

EDGAR. You don't know that! I'm very unpredictable.

VINNY. No, you're not.

EDGAR. Well, I'm — I can sometimes — if I really wanted to — So anyway, what did you guys do while you were tripping?

ASUNCION. *(Suppressing a laugh.)* Um, Mr. Vinny, you want to take this one?

VINNY. We may or may not have jumped on the train tracks.

EDGAR. Jesus!

ASUNCION. Yes, and we may or may not have ridden a freight train down to — where did we go? —

VINNY. — Cortland.

EDGAR. What?!

ASUNCION. Right, Cortland, isn't it such a cute little town?

EDGAR. I've never been there.

ASUNCION. Oh my God, Edgar, you have to go! But go during the day. Anyway, we had to get back to Binghamton —

VINNY. So we may or may not have hitched a ride —

ASUNCION. With a fucking strange-ass man who totally wanted Vinny.

VINNY. He did not want me, Sunny. He wanted my ass.

ASUNCION. And he almost got it, too.

VINNY. So we may or may not have jumped out of his moving truck and onto the highway.

EDGAR. Who are you people? I don't know either of you.

ASUNCION. So, Edgar, you in for tonight?

EDGAR. Well, you have a good sales pitch, sneaking onto a freight train and getting assaulted by truckers.

ASUNCION. Come on, Edgar! It's gonna be fun!

EDGAR. I'll do it if Vinny wants me to do it. I don't want you to do me any favors.

VINNY. Fucking do it if you want to. Or don't. It doesn't matter.

EDGAR. Okay, I'll do it!

ASUNCION. Awesome! You're gonna be so great!

EDGAR. *(To Vinny.)* If I do it, though, you have to promise you're not going to be mean to me.

VINNY. Shut up, Edgar.

ASUNCION. I'm cutting up ginger! *(Asuncion crosses into the kitchen, Edgar moves to Vinny.)*

EDGAR. I'm fun, Vinny.

VINNY. Relax, Edgar.

EDGAR. I want to be fun.

VINNY. Relax, Edgar. *(Blackout.)*

Scene 2

That night.

Vinny and Asuncion sit peacefully on the couch. They are tripping. Their hands are touching slightly.

ASUNCION. I don't have a fear of mice.
VINNY. That's awesome.
ASUNCION. Did you ever have that dream where you wake up in your bedroom and you stand up on your carpet, but your carpet starts moving because there are so many mice crawling underneath it?
VINNY. I don't have carpeting in my bedroom.
ASUNCION. I dream it all the time. I stand on the carpet and it begins like moving, you know? Like it's alive, kind of. And the mice start crawling out from under the carpeting. And one time, I tried to pick up the mice, you know to like save them. Like put them outside in their natural habistates. But my fingernails started growing, like really quick, and they weren't curling like normal, they were sharpening and becoming flat, like swords or, I don't even know — every thought is in my head right now! And I wanted to save the mice but when I picked them up, I just stabbed them to death. I tried to pick them up just with the middle part of my hand but they would just get caught on my nails and slide down them, stabbed. And I start crying and breathing and I feel so sad for the little mice and their little folded ears and cold noses. And the more I saved them, the more I killed them. And there was blood and mice all over the bedroom. And when I woke up I had scratched my whole body. *(Edgar bolts out from the bathroom, wearing long yellow rubber cleaning gloves. He is also tripping.)*
EDGAR. I just have one question for all y'all — Where's my fucking OJ at?! *(Asuncion and Vinny stare at him.)* I said, where's my fucking OJ, you stupid motherfuckaz?!
VINNY. You don't sound like that woman.
EDGAR. *(Falsetto.)* My fucking OJ!
ASUNCION. Yeah, you don't sound like her, Edgar.
EDGAR. Okay.

VINNY. Finish cleaning the bathroom.

EDGAR. Okay. *(Edgar exits back into the bathroom.)*

VINNY. *(Pause.)* Edgar told me you like Mariah Carey.

ASUNCION. She's cool, yeah.

VINNY. He said she's your hero. Or heroine, as the case may be.

ASUNCION. I love my heroin!

VINNY. Does Edgar ask you a lot of questions?

ASUNCION. Kind of. But he's sweet. He's like my little koala bear baby brother.

VINNY. Yeah, he's adorable. Hey, Edgar! Edgar! Could you come back out here? *(Edgar reenters with his yellow gloves.)* Edgar, Sunny was just telling me about Mariah Carey.

EDGAR. *(Wasted.)* When are we going to the train, muthafuckas?

VINNY. We'll go in a minute.

EDGAR. 'Cause the bathroom is — and I can't believe I've never noticed this before — *(A British accent.)* ah-filthy!

ASUNCION. I am not riding a train right now.

EDGAR. Oh, come on, Asuncion, you never want to do anything fun!

VINNY. Hey, Edgar, Sunny told me an interesting dream she had about mice! Maybe you should write it down!

EDGAR. What are you saying?

VINNY. I think it says something interesting about her subconscious.

EDGAR. Shut up, Vinny. Asuncion, isn't it cool that we're gonna know each other forever?

ASUNCION. I'm gonna be a really old-looking grandma. *(Edgar holds Asuncion's hand. Vinny swipes him away.)*

VINNY. I think the story would interest you. Maybe you could write a chapter about mice!

EDGAR. Shut up, Vinny. I mean, think about it — someday, Asuncion, someday your kids and my kids are going to be like best friends.

VINNY. Not if they're anything like you.

EDGAR. Shut up, Vinny! And they'll have joint birthday parties and Stuart and I will watch football!

VINNY. You've never watched football in your life.

EDGAR. And you and my wife will go shopping at Macy's and we'll all eat dinner and shower together and it will be great and we'll be best friends! — *(Vinny pulls out Edgar's notebook from under the couch and little scraps of paper come flying out.)*

41

VINNY. Hey, look what I found! What is this?

EDGAR. Vinny!

VINNY. Edgar, why don't you show Asuncion what you've been writing about her? *(Edgar runs to Vinny and covers his mouth. Vinny shoves him back and picks up the papers.)* About how she's a mail-order bride — a whore!

ASUNCION. What?

VINNY. About how she got her green card in exchange for semen.

ASUNCION. What are you talking about?

EDGAR. I am not writing anything. Vinny, shut the fuck up!

VINNY. *(Picking up a scrap.)* Look at this one! "Ate a frozen waffle." That one's kind of boring, don't you think, Edgar? Couldn't get some better field notes?!

ASUNCION. What the hell's going on here?

EDGAR. Nothing!

VINNY. "Thinks Neil Armstrong was a president." Now that one's good. That's fucking funny.

EDGAR. Vinny! What are you doing to me!?

VINNY. "Tried to play chess. Alone."

ASUNCION. Stop it!

VINNY. See, Edgar, now it's all out in the open. Ask her anything you want.

EDGAR. Asuncion, I'm not ... writing anything about you.

ASUNCION. What do you think I am?

EDGAR. Well, I don't know. But I'm not judging!

ASUNCION. You think I'm a prostitute?

EDGAR. Are you? Is she?

VINNY. Ask her!

EDGAR. Are you?

ASUNCION. I'm your brother's wife.

EDGAR. I'm sure it's a very complicated arrangement.

ASUNCION. Do you really think I'm a prostitute, Edgar?

EDGAR. I don't know what you are!

ASUNCION. Why would you think that?

EDGAR. Because of ... clues! But I love you for who you are! On the inside! But I am also very curious! Are you? *(Asuncion picks up Edgar's notebook and walks into the bedroom, closing the door.)* Asuncion! Please don't read that! I'm sorry! I'm not sure what's going on right now! Asuncion, please come back out! Vinny, I hate you, I think!

VINNY. No, you don't.

EDGAR. Asuncion. Please come back out. Asuncion! I hate you, Vinny, so much.

VINNY. No, you don't. *(Beat.)* You want to suck my dick?

EDGAR. What?

VINNY. I asked you if you wanted to suck my dick.

EDGAR. Why would you ask me that?

VINNY. 'Cause you fucking act like it.

EDGAR. Well, you're my mentor. And my best friend.

VINNY. So I'm asking you. Do you want to suck my dick?

EDGAR. You're my best friend. In the whole world.

VINNY. The whole wide world?

EDGAR. Yeah.

VINNY. It's a big fucking place. I'm honored.

EDGAR. *(Mumbles absently.)* What the hell is going on right about now? *(Edgar begins to walk toward Vinny as Asuncion enters.)*

ASUNCION. Edgar …

EDGAR. Yes, ma'am?

VINNY. Asuncion! Just in time to show Edgar how to perform fellatio. It's a delicate art and who better to teach the young man than someone who does it professionally.

ASUNCION. Edgar, do you really think that of me?

EDGAR. I'm an open-minded person. I believe anything is possible. And that you should reach for the stars. Because even if you don't grab one, you still tried!

ASUNCION. Go clean the bathroom. *(Edgar goes back into the bathroom. We hear him puking.)*

VINNY. We're just fucking around.

ASUNCION. You … you don't think that about me. Do you?

VINNY. I do; I think you're one of the greatest whores in the world. Come here. *(Asuncion sits next to Vinny on the couch. She lies down, with her feet in his lap. He holds them sweetly, like a brother.)*

ASUNCION. You're an asshole, Vinny.

VINNY. And you're a cunt, nice to meet you. *(Edgar storms out of the bathroom —)*

EDGAR. And another thing!

VINNY. And here's the taint! Hey, taint!

EDGAR. And another thing! Asuncion, why do you hang out with Vinny so much!

VINNY. Because she likes me.

EDGAR. I'm not asking you! Asuncion, why do you hang out with Vinny so much?

ASUNCION. Because I like him.

EDGAR. But you're my sister-in-law! Why don't you like me?

ASUNCION. *(Simply.)* Because you're selfish, Edgar.

EDGAR. I maybe have bad social skills.

ASUNCION. Nope.

EDGAR. You guys are just closer in age is all!

ASUNCION. *(Simple.)* No, you're just selfish.

EDGAR. No, I'm not. I'm not selfish. All I think about is other people.

VINNY. You are kind of selfish, Edgar.

EDGAR. YOU? You think I'm selfish? I do everything for you.

VINNY. You're staying in my apartment!

EDGAR. *(Kneels down before Vinny.)* But I serve you. I just want to serve you, Vinny, so much!

ASUNCION. Get up Edgar.

EDGAR. I love you, Vinny. You were my favorite teacher. Did I ever tell you that?

VINNY. I was your teaching assistant.

EDGAR. My whole life, I loved you.

VINNY. I met you when you were an undergrad.

EDGAR. I know! *(Asuncion stands up and goes to the kitchen, leaving the boys alone.)*

ASUNCION. You're both acting like children! Edgar, I'm making you ginger tea. Vinny, don't open a window, he'll jump.

EDGAR. And maybe I will! *(Intimately.)* Vinny, I think of you like my idol, like who I want to be when I'm you.

VINNY. That's nice.

EDGAR. And I love you, Vinny. And I don't know how to prove that to you. Maybe I should do … what you asked me to do.

VINNY. You want to suck my dick?

EDGAR. Well, stop saying those words, it makes it sound crude, but maybe as a nice thing. Maybe I could just do it nice and gentle and it will just be nice, like if we shook hands for a long time.

VINNY. Except with my dick in your mouth.

EDGAR. Please, it sounds crude.

ASUNCION. Okay, this is fucked up. It's enough, Vinny!

VINNY. We're just shaking hands, Asuncion.

ASUNCION. Whoa — Edgar, don't do anything.

VINNY. Shut up, Asuncion.

ASUNCION. Vinny, he's never done acid before. He doesn't know what he's doing.

EDGAR. I think I'll be okay. I feel okay.

ASUNCION. Edgar, get off the fucking floor.

VINNY. Yo, shut the fuck up, Asuncion!

ASUNCION. Edgar! *(Asuncion walks to the boys to break them up. Vinny shoves her back.)* Vinny! *(She tries again but Vinny shoves her back, harder.)* EDGAR!

VINNY. Shut the fuck up! *(Asuncion walks to the kitchen, takes the pot off the stove, brings it to the boys and douses them with the hot water. Edgar snaps up.)*

EDGAR. Oh God! What happened? What's going on! *(Edgar punches Vinny in the stomach.)*

VINNY. Oof! Fuck, Jesus, Edgar!

EDGAR. What did we do? What did we do? *(Edgar punches Vinny in the stomach again and again.)* I'm sorry. *(Vinny sits on the couch in pain. He pulls up his pants.)* Sorry about that, Vinny. *(Vinny stands up slowly. Then, in one swift motion, he decks Edgar in the chest. Edgar crumbles to the floor.)*

ASUNCION. Vinny!

VINNY. *(Whisper.)* Shh. The neighbors. *(Vinny stands up and calmly walks into his bedroom as the lights begin to fade. Asuncion slaps Edgar to make sure he's awake.)*

ASUNCION. Edgar. Edgar!

EDGAR. *(Mumbles.)* You're not a hooker?

ASUNCION. Go to sleep, Edgar.

EDGAR. *(Mumbles.)* I had a — I had a whole thing planned —

ASUNCION. Go to sleep. *(Edgar passes out, still wearing the yellow gloves. Blackout.)*

Scene 3

The next morning.

Light streams in through the central window. The house is still a mess.

Edgar lies in the same place, face down, still wearing the yellow cleaning gloves. Asuncion sleeps on the couch.

The apartment buzzer rings. It rings again.

Edgar stumbles up, buzzes the intercom, and walks back to the floor.

EDGAR. *(Mumbling to no one.)* Sure, come on in … *(Edgar passes out on the floor again. After a moment, Stuart enters the apartment. He pauses, taking everything in: the ransacked house, his brother passed out on the floor and his wife on the couch. Stuart moves to Asuncion, checks her and strokes her head. Stuart picks up the pot and brings it to the stove. He grabs the pillows from the floor and puts them on the couch. He walks in to the bathroom and then crosses back to Asuncion.)*
STUART. *(Whispers sweetly.)* Sunny. Sunny!
ASUNCION. I wanna go home.
STUART. Are you okay?
ASUNCION. I want to go home. I don't care who's there. I wanna go home.
STUART. We're gonna be fine.
ASUNCION. We are?
STUART. We'll be home in three hours. *(Edgar stirs awake and ambles into the bathroom. Stuart and Asuncion wait for him. Edgar enters from the bathroom and sees his brother.)*
EDGAR. Morning, asshole.
STUART. Your house is a mess, man. With the exception of the bathroom, which was spotless.
EDGAR. What are you doing here?

STUART. I'm here to get Asuncion. And to thank you. *(Stuart pulls out a check from his pocket.)* Here's some money for your troubles. You can split this with Vinny. *(Edgar looks at the check. And tears it up dramatically.)* Jesus, Edgar!

EDGAR. I don't need your pity money! *(Beat.)* Yes, I do. I'm broke. That was rash, sorry. Can I have another check, please?

STUART. I don't have my checkbook.

EDGAR. Well, what do you have on you? Cash-wise.

STUART. *(Searching through his wallet.)* I have fifty bucks. Sunny, you have anything?

ASUNCION. I have like two hundred —

EDGAR. Two hundred fifty, that's fine. Thanks. *(Edgar grabs her money.)* Is this hooker money?

ASUNCION. Shut the fuck up, Edgar.

STUART. What's hooker money?

ASUNCION. Your brother decided that I was a prostitute.

STUART. What? What did you do to her, Edgar?

EDGAR. Nothing.

ASUNCION. He didn't do anything to me. He just thinks I'm a hooker.

STUART. Why would you think she's a hooker?

EDGAR. Or a mail-order bride or something. So what are you?

ASUNCION. What do you mean, what am I?

EDGAR. You're from the Philippines!

ASUNCION. So?

EDGAR. It's a poor country.

ASUNCION. Right?

EDGAR. And in poor countries people do what they need to do to get by. It's terrible.

STUART. Okay…?

EDGAR. And you're a stockbroker.

STUART. I am.

EDGAR. And a lot of times, wealthy men get mail-order brides. And she's … *(To Asuncion.)* You're so beautiful.

ASUNCION. Thank you.

EDGAR. No, you're really beautiful, Asuncion. I mean, your face is beautiful, it makes you look like you're a nice person too, not just pretty. And Stuart, you're fat, kind of.

STUART. No, I'm not.

ASUNCION. It's okay, I like fat men.

STUART. But I'm not fat.

EDGAR. You have a gut. Like the gut of a guy who buys his wife. *(Stammers.)* And I just figured she's from the slums of Manila so —

STUART. She's not.

ASUNCION. I told you, Edgar, I'm from Makati. Not the slums. My parents were rich.

EDGAR. But you told me your mother died.

ASUNCION. She did, I have an inheritance.

EDGAR. So what are you doing here then?! In America!

ASUNCION. I'm not allowed to come to America?

EDGAR. Well, it depends what you're doing here! We can't just tolerate immigration willy-nilly!

ASUNCION. I came here for business!

EDGAR. What kind of business?

STUART. You're being an asshole, Edgar.

EDGAR. Well, at least someone is. I'm looking out for my nation!

STUART. Sunny, why don't you go pack your stuff.

ASUNCION. Thank you. *(Crosses to Edgar.)* I'm sorry I couldn't help you more, Edgar. *(She brushes past him into the bedroom.)*

EDGAR. So, if she's not a hooker, why did she have to stay up here? What did you rope her into doing?

STUART. I didn't rope her into anything.

EDGAR. So what was it?

STUART. I'm not telling you. You're a child.

EDGAR. *(Smug.)* Well, I know it was something illegal.

STUART. Oh yeah? You do?

EDGAR. Yeah! You were probably covering up a mass slaughter in the Middle East so you could extract cheap oil.

STUART. You're an idiot!

EDGAR. Or running a child labor crime ring in your basement.

STUART. Okay, shut up. You wanna know what it was?

EDGAR. Yes!

STUART. Her family's been selling cheap antibiotics from the Philippines. It's their family business and Sunny's been trying to get out of it! And she couldn't be in New York while I cleaned up the last of this bullshit.

EDGAR. So why wouldn't you tell me that!?

STUART. Because you're a child. I just didn't realize how young!

EDGAR. Okay, well then, I'm gonna turn her in.

STUART. No, you're not.

EDGAR. How do you know?

STUART. Because you don't do things like that. You don't do much of anything.

EDGAR. I do lots of things.

STUART. You don't do anything, Edgar.

EDGAR. I went to Cambodia!

STUART. Would you shut the fuck up about Cambodia! You went there by accident. For two fucking nights.

EDGAR. Doesn't matter. I went there!

STUART. Yeah, when your little freshman spring break plane to Bangkok got rerouted.

EDGAR. Well, where have you gone? I mean what difficult places have you been to?

STUART. This apartment ranks pretty high. Is that your gauge of a person's value? Where they travel?

EDGAR. Not value, but I do think it's important. We're too ethnocentric in America, I've always said that.

STUART. But you think you're better than me!

EDGAR. Well, I am!

STUART. No, we're just different!

EDGAR. Why are you attacking my convictions?

STUART. You don't have convictions, Edgar. You have opinions. They're two very different things. Sit down! *(Edgar sits.)* I took Asuncion up here because she wanted to meet her new brother. Yes, we were in a bit of trouble, which is my issue — not yours! — but when I told her I thought she should stay in a hotel for a few days, she starts crying, thinking that my white family won't accept my new Filipina bride. And I understood why. Because, frankly, white people have kind of been pricks over the years. But whatever you did to her this week, however you made her feel, makes you the worst kind of white prick there is. Because you call yourself a pussy, when you're actually a prick! *(Edgar is stunned on the couch. Vinny coughs awake and stumbles in.)*

VINNY. Hey, man.

STUART. Morning, Vinny.

VINNY. Thanks for showing up unannounced again. *(Vinny crosses into the bathroom and leaves the door open as he pisses. Edgar exits into the bedroom as Asuncion reenters.)*

STUART. We're gonna go. You ready?

ASUNCION. One sec. Toothbrush. *(She walks into the bathroom to fetch her toothbrush as Vinny reenters —)*

49

VINNY. Everything cool?

STUART. We're gonna be fine.

VINNY. Wow. Congratulations, brother.

STUART. I can fucking breathe again. *(Asuncion enters with her toiletries.)*

ASUNCION. I'm ready.

STUART. Cool. Edgar, we're leaving. You want to come say good-bye?

ASUNCION. Edgar, come say goodbye to me. *(Edgar does not come out.)*

STUART. It's okay, don't worry about him. I'll call you, Edgar. Let's go, come on, honey. *(Vinny tries to pull Asuncion into a hug, but she resists.)*

VINNY. Sunny! I'm gonna miss you.

ASUNCION. Thanks, Vinny.

VINNY. I'm glad we got to know each other.

ASUNCION. Tell Edgar I said goodbye to him.

STUART. We got a spare room, anytime you want, man. You should come down and visit, you don't even have to call.

VINNY. Yeah, maybe. If I'm in the neighborhood and especially if I got no fuckin' OJ! *(Stuart exits with Asuncion without acknowledging Vinny. To himself, in a Brooklyn accent.)* I'm right fresh outta OJ! *(Vinny walks into the bathroom and turns on the shower. He reenters, whistling, as Edgar finally emerges.)*

EDGAR. The water's running.

VINNY. I'm waiting for it to warm up.

EDGAR. It warms up immediately here. *(Quiet.)* You knew about them?

VINNY. Yeah.

EDGAR. She's not a mail-order bride.

VINNY. I know.

EDGAR. You didn't tell me.

VINNY. No.

EDGAR. Why?

VINNY. "If you gotta ask, you're never gonna know."

EDGAR. Louis Armstrong.

VINNY. *(Nods.)* Sure, man.

EDGAR. No one told me anything.

VINNY. I know.

EDGAR. No one ever tells me anything. I feel silly right now.

VINNY. I'm taking a shower. Then I have a class. I'll be home late. You should go somewhere, Edgar.
EDGAR. I will.
VINNY. I mean you should go somewhere. Edgar. *(Vinny exits to the bathroom. Edgar stares after him. Blackout.)*

Scene 4

That night.

Edgar is on his laptop. Vinny enters, from work.

VINNY. I've given up marijuana. It was a crutch. And it coats the lungs with cancer. Everything gives you cancer. What a fucking nightmare. I'm going to start taking better care of myself. Maybe I'll buy us a new bike. *(Vinny notices Edgar.)* Are you alright? *(Edgar does not look up. Plainly.)* Have I done something to upset you? *(Edgar ignores him and types on the computer.)* What are you doing?
EDGAR. I spent the day looking for plane tickets to Dar es Salaam.
VINNY. Good, Edgar, that's good.
EDGAR. In Tanzania.
VINNY. I know where it is.
EDGAR. I actually found a way to get there for 196 dollars. That's the cheapest way.
VINNY. Are you going to buy a ticket?
EDGAR. I could for 196 dollars. You leave out of Logan, so I would have to take the bus up to Boston, but I could take the Chinatown bus for fifteen dollars, so that's, you know, do-able. From Boston you fly to Manchester, England on Virgin Airlines, there's a special if you stay in Manchester for a weekend. Then you take Cathay Pacific Airlines to Dubai, and there would be a seven-hour layover, which is not a big deal for me but then it gets a little weird. For some reason, if you fly through Muscat, Oman and into Mogadishu on Royal Air Moroc, you can catch a red-eye if you're quick, because the layover is only fifteen minutes, into Cape Town

and then an eight-hour flight the next day on Ethiopia Airlines, which has a lousy safety record, into Dar es Salaam, Tanzania. *(Pause.)* I've just been sitting here all day trying every possible combination. To find the cheapest way in.

VINNY. Looks like you found a good one.

EDGAR. They're a beautiful people, have you seen pictures?

VINNY. Well, I just got home.

EDGAR. Look. *(Edgar tilts his computer to show Vinny the Tanzanians.)* Stunning people, huh?

VINNY. A little thin.

EDGAR. Don't joke, there's a shortage of food. Aren't they stunning?

VINNY. They're remarkable.

EDGAR. So dark.

VINNY. No white blood.

EDGAR. They're majestic almost. And miserable, I want to weep for them.

VINNY. They're not weeping for you, I can promise you that.

EDGAR. Doesn't matter. I will for them.

VINNY. So, are you going to Dar Es Salaam?

EDGAR. It's 196 dollars. I could afford it.

VINNY. Right. That's true. But then you wouldn't have much money left.

EDGAR. Oh.

VINNY. And what if you get a disease there? How are you gonna pay for that?

EDGAR. What kind of disease?

VINNY. Malaria. Dengue. Yellow fever. Drink the wrong cup of water and, three months later, a worm crawls out of your body.

EDGAR. Well, if I got a disease, maybe I deserved it — maybe it would be character-building.

VINNY. Could be. *(Beat.)* But I don't want to have to go all the way over there to drag your sick ass home and nurse you back to life.

EDGAR. I'm sure there are doctors in Tanzania.

VINNY. Maybe. It's too bad you're going to Tanzania. Finals are coming up and I was hoping you could grade some papers for me.

EDGAR. Really?

VINNY. Yeah. But you'll be in Tanzania.

EDGAR. Right. *(Vinny tousles Edgar's bangs —)*

VINNY. Cool. Listen, I'm gonna jump into a shower, but I'm gonna go to Frankie's after? Get a sandwich. You wanna come with?

EDGAR. Okay.

VINNY. Great. I'll be out in fifteen minutes, get ready, dudette. You hungry?

EDGAR. A little.

VINNY. Good, I'm famished! *(Vinny walks off to the bathroom and we hear the shower turn on. He begins whistling in the shower. Edgar slowly closes his computer and then turns toward the bathroom. Blackout.)*

End of Play

PROPERTY LIST

Pan-African flag
Casio keyboard
Joint
Bicycle
Glass of water
Towel
Wallet
Cell phone
Book
Glass of water
Duffle bag
Bag of McDonald's food
BlackBerry
Joint, papers, lighter
Notepad and pen
Pot of water
Mug
Purse with bag of tea and cell phone
Piece of paper
Small tape recorder
iPod
Djembe
Scrap paper, Post-Its
Bag of bagels
Pen, napkin
Check
Wallet with cash
Toothbrush
Laptop

SOUND EFFECTS

Cell phone ring, "Fur Elise"
Door buzzer
BlackBerry buzzer
Shower
Pop music
Motorcycle

NEW PLAYS

★ **MOTHERHOOD OUT LOUD by Leslie Ayvazian, Brooke Berman, David Cale, Jessica Goldberg, Beth Henley, Lameece Issaq, Claire LaZebnik, Lisa Loomer, Michele Lowe, Marco Pennette, Theresa Rebeck, Luanne Rice, Annie Weisman and Cheryl L. West, conceived by Susan R. Rose and Joan Stein.** When entrusting the subject of motherhood to such a dazzling collection of celebrated American writers, what results is a joyous, moving, hilarious, and altogether thrilling theatrical event. "Never fails to strike both the funny bone and the heart." *–BackStage.* "Packed with wisdom, laughter, and plenty of wry surprises." *–TheaterMania.* [1M, 3W] ISBN: 978-0-8222-2589-8

★ **COCK by Mike Bartlett.** When John takes a break from his boyfriend, he accidentally meets the girl of his dreams. Filled with guilt and indecision, he decides there is only one way to straighten this out. "[A] brilliant and blackly hilarious feat of provocation." *–Independent.* "A smart, prickly and rewarding view of sexual and emotional confusion." *–Evening Standard.* [3M, 1W] ISBN: 978-0-8222-2766-3

★ **F. Scott Fitzgerald's THE GREAT GATSBY adapted for the stage by Simon Levy.** Jay Gatsby, a self-made millionaire, passionately pursues the elusive Daisy Buchanan. Nick Carraway, a young newcomer to Long Island, is drawn into their world of obsession, greed and danger. "Levy's combination of narration, dialogue and action delivers most of what is best in the novel." *–Seattle Post-Intelligencer.* "A beautifully crafted interpretation of the 1925 novel which defined the Jazz Age." *–London Free Press.* [5M, 4W] ISBN: 978-0-8222-2727-4

★ **LONELY, I'M NOT by Paul Weitz.** At an age when most people are discovering what they want to do with their lives, Porter has been married and divorced, earned seven figures as a corporate "ninja," and had a nervous breakdown. It's been four years since he's had a job or a date, and he's decided to give life another shot. "Critic's pick!" *–NY Times.* "An enjoyable ride." *–NY Daily News.* [3M, 3W] ISBN: 978-0-8222-2734-2

★ **ASUNCION by Jesse Eisenberg.** Edgar and Vinny are not racist. In fact, Edgar maintains a blog condemning American imperialism, and Vinny is three-quarters into a Ph.D. in Black Studies. When Asuncion becomes their new roommate, the boys have a perfect opportunity to demonstrate how open-minded they truly are. "Mr. Eisenberg writes lively dialogue that strikes plenty of comic sparks." *–NY Times.* "An almost ridiculously enjoyable portrait of slacker trauma among would-be intellectuals." *–Newsday.* [2M, 2W] ISBN: 978-0-8222-2630-7

DRAMATISTS PLAY SERVICE, INC.
440 Park Avenue South, New York, NY 10016 212-683-8960 Fax 212-213-1539
postmaster@dramatists.com www.dramatists.com

NEW PLAYS

★ **THE PICTURE OF DORIAN GRAY by Roberto Aguirre-Sacasa, based on the novel by Oscar Wilde.** Preternaturally handsome Dorian Gray has his portrait painted by his college classmate Basil Hallwood. When their mutual friend Henry Wotton offers to include it in a show, Dorian makes a fateful wish—that his portrait should grow old instead of him—and strikes an unspeakable bargain with the devil. [5M, 2W] ISBN: 978-0-8222-2590-4

★ **THE LYONS by Nicky Silver.** As Ben Lyons lies dying, it becomes clear that he and his wife have been at war for many years, and his impending demise has brought no relief. When they're joined by their children all efforts at a sentimental goodbye to the dying patriarch are soon abandoned. "Hilariously frank, clear-sighted, compassionate and forgiving." *–NY Times.* "Mordant, dark and rich." *–Associated Press.* [3M, 3W] ISBN: 978-0-8222-2659-8

★ **STANDING ON CEREMONY by Mo Gaffney, Jordan Harrison, Moisés Kaufman, Neil LaBute, Wendy MacLeod, José Rivera, Paul Rudnick, and Doug Wright, conceived by Brian Shnipper.** Witty, warm and occasionally wacky, these plays are vows to the blessings of equality, the universal challenges of relationships and the often hilarious power of love. "CEREMONY puts a human face on a hot-button issue and delivers laughter and tears rather than propaganda." *–BackStage.* [3M, 3W] ISBN: 978-0-8222-2654-3

★ **ONE ARM by Moisés Kaufman, based on the short story and screenplay by Tennessee Williams.** Ollie joins the Navy and becomes the lightweight boxing champion of the Pacific Fleet. Soon after, he loses his arm in a car accident, and he turns to hustling to survive. "[A] fast, fierce, brutally beautiful stage adaptation." *–NY Magazine.* "A fascinatingly lurid, provocative and fatalistic piece of theater." *–Variety.* [7M, 1W] ISBN: 978-0-8222-2564-5

★ **AN ILIAD by Lisa Peterson and Denis O'Hare.** A modern-day retelling of Homer's classic. Poetry and humor, the ancient tale of the Trojan War and the modern world collide in this captivating theatrical experience. "Shocking, glorious, primal and deeply satisfying." *–Time Out NY.* "Explosive, altogether breathtaking." *–Chicago Sun-Times.* [1M] ISBN: 978-0-8222-2687-1

★ **THE COLUMNIST by David Auburn.** At the height of the Cold War, Joe Alsop is the nation's most influential journalist, beloved, feared and courted by the Washington world. But as the '60s dawn and America undergoes dizzying change, the intense political dramas Joe is embroiled in become deeply personal as well. "Intensely satisfying." *–Bloomberg News.* [5M, 2W] ISBN: 978-0-8222-2699-4

DRAMATISTS PLAY SERVICE, INC.
440 Park Avenue South, New York, NY 10016 212-683-8960 Fax 212-213-1539
postmaster@dramatists.com www.dramatists.com

NEW PLAYS

★ **BENGAL TIGER AT THE BAGHDAD ZOO by Rajiv Joseph.** The lives of two American Marines and an Iraqi translator are forever changed by an encounter with a quick-witted tiger who haunts the streets of war-torn Baghdad. "[A] boldly imagined, harrowing and surprisingly funny drama." –*NY Times.* "Tragic yet darkly comic and highly imaginative." –*CurtainUp.* [5M, 2W] ISBN: 978-0-8222-2565-2

★ **THE PITMEN PAINTERS by Lee Hall, inspired by a book by William Feaver.** Based on the triumphant true story, a group of British miners discover a new way to express themselves and unexpectedly become art-world sensations. "Excitingly ambiguous, in-the-moment theater." –*NY Times.* "Heartfelt, moving and deeply politicized." –*Chicago Tribune.* [5M, 2W] ISBN: 978-0-8222-2507-2

★ **RELATIVELY SPEAKING by Ethan Coen, Elaine May and Woody Allen.** In TALKING CURE, Ethan Coen uncovers the sort of insanity that can only come from family. Elaine May explores the hilarity of passing in GEORGE IS DEAD. In HONEYMOON MOTEL, Woody Allen invites you to the sort of wedding day you won't forget. "Firecracker funny." –*NY Times.* "A rollicking good time." –*New Yorker.* [8M, 7W] ISBN: 978-0-8222-2394-8

★ **SONS OF THE PROPHET by Stephen Karam.** If to live is to suffer, then Joseph Douaihy is more alive than most. With unexplained chronic pain and the fate of his reeling family on his shoulders, Joseph's health, sanity, and insurance premium are on the line. "Explosively funny." –*NY Times.* "At once deep, deft and beautifully made." –*New Yorker.* [5M, 3W] ISBN: 978-0-8222-2597-3

★ **THE MOUNTAINTOP by Katori Hall.** A gripping reimagination of events the night before the assassination of the civil rights leader Dr. Martin Luther King, Jr. "An ominous electricity crackles through the opening moments." –*NY Times.* "[A] thrilling, wild, provocative flight of magical realism." –*Associated Press.* "Crackles with theatricality and a humanity more moving than sainthood." –*NY Newsday.* [1M, 1W] ISBN: 978-0-8222-2603-1

★ **ALL NEW PEOPLE by Zach Braff.** Charlie is 35, heartbroken, and just wants some time away from the rest of the world. Long Beach Island seems to be the perfect escape until his solitude is interrupted by a motley parade of misfits who show up and change his plans. "Consistently and sometimes sensationally funny." –*NY Times.* "A morbidly funny play about the trendy new existential condition of being young, adorable, and miserable." –*Variety.* [2M, 2W] ISBN: 978-0-8222-2562-1

DRAMATISTS PLAY SERVICE, INC.
440 Park Avenue South, New York, NY 10016 212-683-8960 Fax 212-213-1539
postmaster@dramatists.com   www.dramatists.com

NEW PLAYS

★ **CLYBOURNE PARK by Bruce Norris.** WINNER OF THE 2011 PULITZER PRIZE AND 2012 TONY AWARD. Act One takes place in 1959 as community leaders try to stop the sale of a home to a black family. Act Two is set in the same house in the present day as the now predominantly African-American neighborhood battles to hold its ground. "Vital, sharp-witted and ferociously smart." –*NY Times.* "A theatrical treasure...Indisputably, uproariously funny." –*Entertainment Weekly.* [4M, 3W] ISBN: 978-0-8222-2697-0

★ **WATER BY THE SPOONFUL by Quiara Alegría Hudes.** WINNER OF THE 2012 PULITZER PRIZE. A Puerto Rican veteran is surrounded by the North Philadelphia demons he tried to escape in the service. "This is a very funny, warm, and yes uplifting play." –*Hartford Courant.* "The play is a combination poem, prayer and app on how to cope in an age of uncertainty, speed and chaos." –*Variety.* [4M, 3W] ISBN: 978-0-8222-2716-8

★ **RED by John Logan.** WINNER OF THE 2010 TONY AWARD. Mark Rothko has just landed the biggest commission in the history of modern art. But when his young assistant, Ken, gains the confidence to challenge him, Rothko faces the agonizing possibility that his crowning achievement could also become his undoing. "Intense and exciting." –*NY Times.* "Smart, eloquent entertainment." –*New Yorker.* [2M] ISBN: 978-0-8222-2483-9

★ **VENUS IN FUR by David Ives.** Thomas, a beleaguered playwright/director, is desperate to find an actress to play Vanda, the female lead in his adaptation of the classic sadomasochistic tale *Venus in Fur.* "Ninety minutes of good, kinky fun." –*NY Times.* "A fast-paced journey into one man's entrapment by a clever, vengeful female." –*Associated Press.* [1M, 1W] ISBN: 978-0-8222-2603-1

★ **OTHER DESERT CITIES by Jon Robin Baitz.** Brooke returns home to Palm Springs after a six-year absence and announces that she is about to publish a memoir dredging up a pivotal and tragic event in the family's history—a wound they don't want reopened. "Leaves you feeling both moved and gratifyingly sated." –*NY Times.* "A genuine pleasure." –*NY Post.* [2M, 3W] ISBN: 978-0-8222-2605-5

★ **TRIBES by Nina Raine.** Billy was born deaf into a hearing family and adapts brilliantly to his family's unconventional ways, but it's not until he meets Sylvia, a young woman on the brink of deafness, that he finally understands what it means to be understood. "A smart, lively play." –*NY Times.* "[A] bright and boldly provocative drama." –*Associated Press.* [3M, 2W] ISBN: 978-0-8222-2751-9

DRAMATISTS PLAY SERVICE, INC.
440 Park Avenue South, New York, NY 10016 212-683-8960 Fax 212-213-1539
postmaster@dramatists.com   www.dramatists.com